BENNIE LAMBERT, Ph. D.

HOW TO

GROW

FROM

NO

BREAK THROUGH ADVERSITY
AND MOVE TO YOUR NEXT LEVEL

© LG Publishing 2012

ISBN# 978-0-9884340-0-4

Cover & Layout Design by Luis Santos, Houston, Texas

Printed in the United States of America

Dedication

Dedicated to the memory of my grandmother,

Sadie Bell Lambert, affectionately known as "Big Mama".

1904 - 1983

Thank You

Thank you to those at Midway High School who told me NO, I would not graduate, but never gave up on me.

Thank you to Baylor University for telling me NO, I was not ready for prime time. . .but gave me my Next Opportunity.

Thank you to McLennan Community College for telling me NO, I wasn't too late to start college.

Thank you to Mom, Dad, and Big Mama for telling me the "good" NO's.

Thank you to Mrs. Louise Brown - my first grade teacher - who believed in me.

Thank you to John and Ruth Belew, who believed so much in my grandmother.

Thank you to Earl Cotton, Jr. who gave me my first job as a grocery sacker.

And finally, an immense and infinite "thank-you" to all teachers and coaches everywhere who invest their hearts, minds, and souls to not only teach but help and encourage every student every day!

Acknowledgements

I owe a debt of gratitude to the folks who took an interest in me and my well-being early in life and today.

CONTENTS

Foreword

I first met Bennie Lambert while speaking at a Baylor University Alumni event several years ago. Bennie was the master of ceremonies and auctioneer for the event. When he stepped up to the podium, his story set the ambiance for the evening. This book is that story. The audience became enthused and engaged in the program. It was evident this young man knew how to play the hand he was dealt and . . . *How to Grow from No.*

Throughout the years I would see Bennie at various educational, charity, and civic events. I can attest to the commitment and gift he has for helping others accomplish their educational goals and pursue their dreams.

How to Grow from No brought back many fond recollections of the times Bennie shared his stories of Big Mama. This book is inspiring and filled with stories and ideas that many people can use to take their life to the next level. I feel almost everyone can find a "Big Mama-like" figure in their life.

I have always been a big believer and supporter of education and hard work. My first professional job assignment, after graduating from college, was working the second shift at my father's grocery business. The business employed 67 workers and 19 of them loaded trucks at night. I was quick to remind my father that I had been to graduate school and completed six years of college, but he insisted that I start by loading the trucks in the evenings. My father showed me how to apply my education, learning from the bottom up, working productively and cooperatively with people and inspiring them. My parents taught me, through their words and their actions, that honesty, integrity, plus respect and concern for others was so important.

Having graduated from a small high school in Cameron, Texas, I can truly say it's not necessarily where you are from, but where you are going that makes the difference. Everybody is from somewhere, but everybody may not have a dream that comes true. However, those who do realize and pursue their dreams and ideas, upon reaching them – recognize they did not get there by themselves. They had mentors along the way.

This book depicts several of those people and encounters from Bennie's life experiences. After reading it, you will see the enormous impact that education and hard work have on an individual's life . . . young or not so young! I am proud to call Bennie a friend and a teammate in educating and leading others to become what they believe they can be. The first chapter of *How to Grow from No*, reads, "I'm not famous, but I have a story to share with you." Wow, what a great motivational story!

-Drayton McLane, Jr.
Chairman, McLane Group
Former Chairman/CEO of the Houston Astros

4

Preface

"Never let the fear of striking out get in your way."

-George Herman "Babe" Ruth

Originally targeted to high school and college students, this is my story of being denied admission to college and told I was not *college* material. I believe there are many people who are or have been in similar circumstances and situations.

This book will help you discover your motivation and keep you on track to get to your next level! I want you to be able to grow from that word *no* and realize there are no limits in your life.

After reading and learning from my experiences, people with challenging circumstances in education, business, sales, government, and athletics will find a renewed awareness and motivation to reach their potential by pursuing their passions.

I graduated from high school near the very bottom of my class. Because I had an inspirational person in my life, I went from graduating at the bottom of my class to earning my bachelor's and master's degrees from Baylor University in Waco, Texas and doctorate degree from Texas A & M University in College Station, Texas.

How to Grow from No will teach you to never accept *no* for an answer but instead to grow from *no* by motivating you to get on track, rejuvenate yourself to get your education, and earn what you deserve pertaining to your higher education and career goals.

I want you to learn and realize, from my experiences, that you already have within and around you what it takes to *break through adversity and grow from no* so you can take your life to the next level.

BENNIE LAMBERT, Ph. D.

1

Humble Beginnings

*"Our lives are defined by our opportunities,
even the ones we miss."*

-Benjamin Button

For years I have traveled around the country speaking to various groups, telling my story - hoping to inspire people to improve their lives, *break through adversity, and grow from no.* Every time I speak, I'm bombarded with requests for *my book.* In the back of my mind I've always known I needed to and wanted to write a book. Year after year, I would jot down notes of things I would someday include in my book. At times I would be inspired and actually write more than notes. Life is busy, and *my book* got pushed to the back burner so that I could tend to my busy day-to-day agenda.

Everyone has a story; I am no different. My name is Bennie Lambert. I am not famous, but I have a story to share with you. As may be true for you, my story has humble beginnings. In the next few chapters, you will see how my experiences helped me move to the next levels of my life. More importantly, I want you to think about the person or persons who have made the significant difference in your life.

I could start this story, "once upon a time", but that is how fairy tales start, and my story is no fairy tale. My story is real. I know because I lived it, and I'm still living it today.

Since we just met, it is important that you get an idea of the background and foundation from which this story will be shared. I had big dreams, opportunities, and changes of plans. As you read about my path, it is my sincere hope that you will find inspiration and encouragement to take the actions necessary to move to *your* next level of success.

As a motivational speaker, success coach, and college administrator, I am privileged to meet scores of people, young and old, who have taken decisive steps to pursue and reach their potential. I intently listen to their dreams, goals, desires, and stories because I'm interested in learning exactly what prompted them to take advantage of following their passions. Some of their stories are heart wrenching, while others are heartwarming. However, their narratives share one common theme: a desire to move from one level to the next.

Every time I work with people or speak to a group of peers, I recount pieces of my own story. My goal is to impart the lessons I learned about opportunity, attitude, and perseverance. When individuals apply these principles, they cease to even consider giving up and move toward their true ambition.

In the pages that follow, you will learn about my successes and my failures. You will read about insurmountable obstacles and misplaced efforts – the common human experience. You will also read about the uncommon resolve of the one person who made the most significant difference in my life, Big Mama, who taught me how to move to *my* next level. I invite you to look in on my life and learn from Big Mama, a few others, and me, how you can progress onward and upward to achieve your very best.

2

Home Team Advantage

"What lies behind you and what lies in front of you, pales in comparison to what lies inside of you."

-Ralph Waldo Emerson

I'm from a little place called McGregor. Have you ever been to a place that felt like everybody knew you and your family? That describes McGregor, which offered a homey, family feel to every aspect of life. For instance, the manager at the grocery store, long before computers were accessible and efficient, knew the exact cost and quantity of every item in his inventory. He remembered when a customer's favorite item was out of stock and would apologize for the inconvenience. Most often, he personally would notify customers when the item arrived.

McGregor had a few other sources of industry besides its

two grocery stores. Gilmore and Davis was a large furniture store that served our town and Central Texas. As kids, when we saw the big trucks pass by, we would try to guess where they were headed and what was inside. We would wave to the drivers, and they would wave back as if they really knew us.

Boney's Livestock Auction Barn was another favorite. On Wednesdays, the ranchers would gather for the weekly livestock auction. My grandfather raised cattle and hogs, so we were there every Wednesday. I can still remember the atmosphere and the aroma. We were a small, close-knit community: sellers, buyers, and auctioneers. As a matter of fact, I spent so much time at the livestock barn that I picked up a keen insight for auctioneering. Not long after high school, I began serving as an auctioneer. Hometown folks would often stop me and ask to hear my auctioneering voice, and I was more than happy to oblige.

The main gathering place was McMullen's Automotive Supply. McMullen's was the place where a man could enjoy a cup of coffee, engage in masculine conversation, and get his car fixed, all at the same time. On Saturdays, the talk was, of course, about last night's football game. On other days, the men talked about anything and everything: town happenings, work-related issues, life experiences, past memories, and even faith and politics. I would go to McMullen's with my father and grandfather to soak up the stories and the wisdom. It was such a great time that men showed up whether or not they needed auto repair; they treasured the fellowship.

This was McGregor, my hometown, and I loved it! There was a special feel to it. Whether you grew up there, stopped by for a visit, or just passed through, it was a great place to be and it was a great place to grow up.

Since I was raised by both my parents and my paternal grandparents, I grew up understanding the importance of love, family support, and relationships. With only two children in the family, my sister Ruby and I received more than enough attention, sometimes much more than enough, to build our confidence and self-esteem.

Throughout our school days, Ruby and I played Peewee football, YMCA basketball, little league baseball and the list goes on. Our dad would pick us up from practice and games no matter how late in the evening. After working on the farm all day, dad would be extremely tired, but he never let us down. He knew how much it meant for us to be part of organized athletics, and he and the rest of the family always supported us by attending our games. We could always look up in the stands and find the entire extended Lambert family rooting and cheering us on.

Looking back with the knowledge of what makes outstanding athletic skill, I realize now that I did not possess it. That was not important to my family. What was important was the opportunity to prepare, practice, participate and give my absolute best as part of the team. These were the reasons my family expressed their love and support for Ruby and me.

They believed that family, like teams, was important, and they poured everything into nurturing strong relationships. I cannot overstate the value of love and family encouragement in my life. They were my foundation – and my launching pad. Ruby and I learned early that our parents merely started our journey. They wanted to launch us further than they could lead us, and with the basis of love and family support firmly in place, they kept us connected physically and mentally to education and school.

For the Lamberts, education was the key and our faith

was king. Mom and dad wanted us in school. They wanted to make sure the doors that were closed to them were open to us. In fact, they attended as many Parent Teacher Association (PTA) meetings as possible. I later learned that while my parents would often receive paperwork and notes the school sent home about important information pertaining to school, they struggled with comprehension and understanding.

Nevertheless, my folks were always there to demonstrate their commitment and willingness to do whatever it took for Ruby and me to be successful. They may not have had the formal education or life experiences of their PTA peers, but they had a relentless dedication to make a difference for the school and for us. As a result of my parent's loyalty and support of the PTA, I received a portion of the PTA college scholarship. I know now that it was because of my parent's dedication and not my academic standing.

18

3

Roots to Routes

"Your roots determine your routes."

-Tavist Smiley

My grandmother, affectionately known as Big Mama, was extremely serious about us getting an education. Giving credit where credit is due, Big Mama was the difference in me making it to the next levels. I have much more to share in the chapters to come why the *Big Mama* in your life, can make the big difference for you.

Within my family, as I researched the family tree and levels of educational attainment, I discovered that my mother and father had earned the highest levels of formal education of anyone in the four generations tracing back to the late 1800's. We called dad the valedictorian and mom, the salutatorian. Understand that between them they had only 11 years of formal education. Dad finished the sixth grade, and mom completed the fifth. They were working before they hit their teen years. Their abbreviated education made my parents even more determined that Ruby and I would excel in our educational journeys.

With that being said, it is critically important that you know, acknowledge, and celebrate your history. You really don't know your history until you get connected to the relatives and stories of your family's history, heritage, and life before you were born.

My grandparents, Big Mama and Granddad, shared their stories of growing up and going to school back in their days so often that I will always remember what they said they experienced when it came to education and school.

Their school story was perhaps like your grandparents or great-grandparents. My sister and I sat through our grandparent's account of walking to school "uphill – both ways." While that should be impossible according to the laws of physics, my grandparents would insist that "things were different back then."

In the early 1900's, my grandparents attended a one-room school house where all classes and all grades were taught by one teacher. They loved school and excelled at their studies. However, because their parents needed them to work the farms, both were only able to complete the third grade. Yet those three years and a lifetime of hard work were enough to instill an understanding of the value of education.

Every day when Ruby and I returned from school, Big Mama would ask, "How was your day at school? What did you learn today?" These conversations took place at the dinner table, a special way to sum up a long, productive day. Faith, food, and fellowship were staples, and Big Mama made sure we were well fed – spiritually, emotionally, intellectually, and physically with delicious homemade food to warm and fill our bellies.

What Big Mama understood and accomplished – despite limited formal education – was amazing. She knew how to conduct a good meeting with her family. Somehow she knew to embrace the same principles used by today's top management gurus seeking maximum input and feedback to obtain desired outcomes and solutions. Big Mama knew that education would yield the most optimum results for her grandchildren and skillfully facilitated the practices that would make it appealing to us through our faith, our daily home-cooked, fabulous food, and family face-time.

The reason Big Mama could yield results to what research shows the most effective people do, was very simple. *She connected!* She connected with me, and as a result, she positively influenced me.

Emphasizing formal education in our household was something that came naturally to Big Mama. It was what Big Mama called *common sense.* Big Mama knew that for us to have a real chance at this thing called education, *common sense* dictated that we attend school and be present in class every day. No excuses. To that end, Big Mama did her part. In my 12 years in public school, elementary, junior high, and high school, I missed a total of two days. I would have gone those two days, but Big Mama's *common sense* told her I really was too sick.

Looking back on those early days of my education, I am reminded of the "amended" postal service credo: neither rain, nor snow, nor sleet, nor 100+ temperatures deep in the heart of Texas kept us from school.

It was as simple as this: School is where you learn; learning takes place daily; therefore, you attend school every single day. The adults in my life didn't need an abundance of formal education to understand this. It was just *common sense*!

24

4

Dreams Happen

"Logic will get you from A to B. Imagination will take you everywhere."

-Albert Einstein

Like most young people, I was influenced by the media growing up. I watched TV shows like *The Andy Griffith Show*, *The Beverly Hillbillies*, *Leave It to Beaver*, *I Love Lucy*, and later, *That's My Mama*, *Sanford and Son*, *The Jefferson's*, *All in the Family*, and *The Cosby Show*. I realized at an early age that I enjoyed laughter, humor, and fun. As a result, I still treasure laughter, a good funny story, and good fun. Some influences make lasting impressions.

I also grew up watching the Dallas Cowboys. Young kids tend to know everything there is to know about their favorite team or player, and try to emulate them. I knew every Dallas Cowboy football team member by name, number, and college of origin: Roger Staubach - #12, The Naval Academy; Drew Pearson - #88, Tulsa University; Bob Lilly - #74, Texas Christian University; Bob Hayes - #22, Florida A & M University; and the list goes on. My favorite player, however, was Cowboy running back, Calvin Hill - #35, Yale University. In my mind, there was no one else like Calvin Hill. He was my role model, and he influenced my dreams.

I discovered later that Calvin Hill and I shared many similarities. We grew up with hardworking, sharecropping fathers who were our biggest fans. Calvin's dad played ball with him after working long days in the field, just as my dad played ball with me when he finished his long hours in the fields. Our fathers instilled in us the value of hard work and proper attitude. Calvin's father died when he was 34; my dad died when I was 33. However as a young follower of Calvin Hill on the football field, I didn't know any of these things about him then. I only knew that he played professional football, and he was a running back.

This was now my big dream. I wanted to be a professional football player. I wanted to be a running back. Was I the professional football player type? Did I have a professional football player's build? These were moot points for me. My hero, Calvin Hill, was a professional football player, and that was enough for me. And so, I dreamed.

My dream was fueled each week at Baylor Stadium, home of the Baylor Bears' football team in Waco, Texas. It was also the workplace of my parents and grandparents, who to earn extra money for the family, served as custodians after the home football games - one of many jobs they managed during my childhood.

Because they believed in hard work at every age, I accompanied them, properly disposing of trash after Saturday home games. I can still remember as a little boy saying to myself, "One day I'm going to play professional football. I'm going to play professional football." As I worked down on the field with my parents and grandparents, I visualized myself as a professional football player. What I didn't realize at my tender age was that it would take more than dreaming or cleaning to make this happen.

My senior year of high school I learned that I had to attend college to play professional football. I figured, *no problem,* and completed my application for admission to Baylor University, the closest university to my hometown and the only college I really knew much about. I submitted the completed admissions package, and that March, final semester of my senior year, I received a cordial letter from Baylor's Dean of Admissions, Mr. Herman D. Thomas:

BAYLOR
UNIVERSITY

Dear Bennie Lambert,

You have honored Baylor by applying for admission, and we sincerely appreciate your interest.

However, due to low test scores and poor class rank, we are unable to admit you to Baylor University's freshman class.

Please contact us if you would like to discuss your application and options further.

Sincerely,

H. D. Thomas,
Dean for Admissions

OFFICE OF ADMISSIONS

I must say, I have never been as embarrassed or ashamed as I was reading that letter. I was disappointed in myself for a lot of reasons, but what made the situation worse was that I'd already leaked my intentions. The word was out that I, Bennie Lambert, was headed to Baylor University.

I don't know how your family works, but in mine, if you wanted to get the word out about what was happening in the family, you told Big Mama. She told everyone else! Naturally, when I applied to Baylor, I told Big Mama - the rest is history. Big Mama was so proud; she literally told everyone.

So bottom line, everyone in my hometown and in my entire family was of the impression that Bennie was headed to college at Baylor University in the fall.

It was heartbreaking to let everyone down. Equally depressing were the green and gold Baylor University Polo shirts and jerseys from relatives and friends sent as graduation gifts after Big Mama had told all that "Bennie was going to Baylor."

As I surveyed my graduation gifts, the Baylor memorabilia was a constant, bittersweet reminder that I had failed. At that point, a Baylor degree – and a professional football career – seemed impossible.

Although I did work at a local grocery store as a part-time grocery sacker, I knew this was not my destiny. Maybe Baylor was out. Maybe professional football was out too. For sure, I didn't know what my future would bring, but I did know I could still dream. I could dream big.

One day while sacking groceries, a customer mentioned the local community college. Back then, I didn't really understand community colleges, thinking they weren't *real college*, just 13th and 14th grades. I didn't know better then, but I sure know better today. Community colleges are one of the best higher education and training opportunities in America. Community colleges connect you to your next levels!

The community college that accepted me and gave me my opportunity in higher education was a place called McLennan Community College in Waco, Texas. I still dreamed of playing professional football, which meant that I had to go to college. McLennan Community College was a college, a real college, too. I wasn't thrilled, however, with the idea of going to a college that didn't even have a football team. How could that path lead me where I wanted to go? I decided to go on faith and a big push from Big Mama.

I had heard that school started August 23rd, which coincidentally was my birthday. When I told Big Mama, she declared we would be at McLennan Community College on that day. We showed up bright and early at the college on the first day of class for the new semester.

There we were, Big Mama and me, standing in line waiting to register. Even though we had arrived at 8 a.m., the lines were unbelievably long. I was surrounded by a sea of faces that looked to be my age. I was getting a little excited, trying to look cool, calm, and collected - until I remembered that I was there with my grandmother. One thing for certain, I could not look *cool* with Big Mama at college with me.

By the grace of God, an advisor pulled us out of line and took us into a room. I am eternally grateful to that advisor. In addition to preventing the destruction of my cool status, she admitted and registered me for community college classes.

I was now officially the first person in my family to start college. Big Mama appeared more excited than I. The look on her face was one of gratitude, elation, and hope. Joyful tears poured from her eyes and streamed down her face. Looking back, I imagine she had come to the revelation that all her hard work and sacrifice were finally paying off. She got to see first hand in her lifetime, her own blood relative, her favorite grandson, Bennie, enroll in college.

The visit with the advisor was eye opening for me. She asked me: "What do you want to be? What do you want to major in?" I had never had to seriously answer those questions in a moment-defining setting, and I had never given them critical thought.

I did remember Big Mama always saying, "Bennie, make something of yourself; be somebody." I turned and asked, "What do you want me to be, Big Mama?" She wanted me to be a doctor. She wanted people to make appointments to see me. She wanted me to make a lot of money for showing up and helping people feel better. I turned back to the advisor and said, "That's what I'd like to be. I want to be a doctor." The advisor built my class schedule accordingly for one who desires to eventually become a doctor. Little did I know, however, that to be a doctor, you needed to like math, and you needed to like science. I hated both. But I concluded since I liked money, I could stick it out.

I went to my first series of classes. I will never forget the day I walked into zoology class. It was a whole new world. I was thrown into a realm of existence with its own language. A horse wasn't just a horse anymore; it was something I couldn't pronounce. I was in trouble!

After about eight weeks, we had our first test. A week or so later, the professor returned the tests. We held our breath. I heard a few sighs, but mine was a prolonged sigh of disappointment. I scored 47 out of 100 points on the test. Although I had another class right after zoology, I didn't bother going. I went straight to the phone to call Big Mama, who was cleaning a family's house.

"Big Mama, this is Bennie."

"Bennie, what's the matter?"

"Big Mama, if you want a doctor in the family, you need to have another grandson."

5

Changes Happen

*"Education is the most powerful weapon,
which you can use to change the world."*

-Nelson Mandela

I changed my mind and major, right then. I hung up the phone and headed towards the area where I initially was admitted and spoke with that advisor who pulled me out of the long line. During that short walk, I had a serious talk with myself. It was probably the first of many serious heart-to-heart talks that I would have with myself.

It was obvious that science was not my strongest subject; it might easily have been my weakest. Something had to change. I walked and wondered: "Bennie, what are you going to do now?" Before I got to my advisor, I had decided to change my major.

I learned two things during my walk that day: 1) you cannot be something that someone else wants you to be; and 2) the people who raise you can influence you greatly without you even knowing it.

Big Mama wanted me to be a physician; however, I lacked the fundamental skills to make that a reality. As much as Big Mama dreamed of her doctor grandchild, the common sense she possessed – and passed on to me – dictated that I had to do something where I could develop a positive interest and learnable skill. I was not skilled in the sciences, and a mastery of the sciences was required to be a doctor. Therefore, I could not and would not become a medical doctor. This reality forced me to look in a different direction.

"When one door closes, another opens; but we often look so long and so regretfully upon the closed door that we do not see the one which has opened for us."

- Alexander G. Bell

Through my formative years, I watched my grandparents run their own businesses. They learned business acumen on the job in three different family ventures. My grandparents were farmers

- sharecroppers. They grew their own food, shared a portion with others, and sold the remainder for profit.

My grandfather was also a skilled carpenter, building five brick homes of 3,000-plus square feet each - brick by brick from the foundation up.

He was a skilled mechanic, as well, who built and repaired automobiles. How's that for providing the necessities of life? That's right - food, shelter, and transportation. Day after day, I watched my grandparents interact with customers, keep the books, pay bills, maintain inventory, and yes, engage in humanitarian efforts.

Having learned the principles of utilizing my God-given resources by watching and working alongside my grandparents, I knew that I had found my calling. I changed course.

For college students, that equates to changing majors. That's okay. Change can be good. Change can be corrective. Change can be life-saving. Changing my mind and my major that early in my college career kept me from wasting precious time. Had I not changed my mind and my major when I did, more than likely, I would have spent countless hours trying to force strength from a place of weakness, a futile and discouraging effort to say the least.

Instead, I understood right then, the next step necessary for me to take it to the next level, was change. Change of mind and change of major would change my opportunity.

Often we are backed into positions where the pressure feels so severe that if we don't live up to someone else's ideals and expectations, we're selling ourselves short. In truth, we are not. I believe that an important principle is: *treat yourself and not cheat yourself*. If you need to adapt in order to treat yourself, do it. If you need to alter to keep from cheating yourself, do it. Don't miss the opportunity to move to the next level because you are not willing to modify - to change.

I didn't know it at the time, but four of my McLennan Community College classes were developmental. That means they were pre-college, designed to improve my sub-par skills in basic reading, English, writing, and math to get my academic skills at college level. It was probably a blessing that I didn't realize this, because when I made my first "A" in a course, I decided I was indeed a successful college student.

That "A" gave me the confidence to take the next step. That "A" did not come easy. I spent extra time in the learning lab being tutored and assisted by people who were there to help.

Lesson: Take advantage of *bonus opportunity*. *Bonus opportunity* is those offerings in life that are always there for us to utilize, but we have to be willing to work around the schedule of others for our benefit. They are there to help and add value to our goals and objectives.

I continued taking classes, and before long, I earned more than 60 transferable college-credit hours, enabling me to apply and be accepted as a transfer student to Baylor University. The community college was my stepping stone to Baylor University, and the opportunity to play football. My dream was back on track. I was at Baylor, and I was playing football . . . sort of.

As I mentioned, like many young people, I was influenced by television. I loved watching TV. During football season, my favorite thing to do was watch the Dallas Cowboys, America's team. My biggest hero was #35, Calvin Hill, and I had every intention of following in his footsteps. Now, here I was at Baylor University, one step closer to being like my hero.

At Baylor, I *walked on* to the football team. That means no college or university valued my athletic talent enough to offer me a scholarship. I was fortunate, though, because Baylor's coach, Grant Teaff, had been a *walk on* himself. He understood the desire to play football. He gave me the same opportunity he had been given. I was on the team!

I didn't understand the life of a *walk on*. Not only is a *walk on* not valued enough to earn a scholarship, but they are used as practice opponents for number one, blue-chip scholarship players. The *walk on* and other non-starters were responsible for preparing the first team for upcoming opponents during practice.

Attempting to emulate my hero, I informed Coach Teaff I was a running back. Amazingly, he didn't have a problem with that, even though I weighed all of 150 pounds. I'll never forget the second day of practice.

We were scrimmaging against the first team, and I was finally given a chance to play in practice. The quarterback pitched me the ball, and I went running. I took about four steps. The next thing I remember was waking up feeling like I had been hit by a freight train.

The guy who hit me eventually broke seven helmets while he was at Baylor. Mine was number three. When I could think clearly again, I discovered the name of the player who hit me. It was none other than future NFL Hall-of-Famer, Mike Singletary. Mike went on to play 12 seasons with the Chicago Bears, garnering a couple of Super Bowl wins in the process.

On that day, the second day of my college football career, I quit. I didn't even check in my uniform. I just never returned for practice. That was enough football for me.

Another plan had changed, but that was okay. I thank God today for that encounter with Mike Singletary. Mike and I became great friends but not because of football. We became great friends because we were business majors at Baylor University.

Although my short-lived college football career forced another change of plans, it created my next opportunity. The level of greatness that I witnessed in Mike Singletary sent me seeking that same level of greatness in my own life. I was determined to find what I had to offer that would make as big an impact on others as Mike had made on me - without the concussion!

6

Paper Travels

*"Formal education will make you a living;
self-education will make you a fortune."*

-Jim Rohn

There are two things on the wall in my parent's home today. The first is that rejection letter from Herman D. Thomas, Dean of Admissions at Baylor University. Right next to that is my Baylor University Bachelor of Business Administration degree. I earned that degree for myself – and for Big Mama. Her dream was to see me walk across that Baylor stage and graduate. Unfortunately, Big Mama passed away two months before my graduation, but she definitely knew I was going to graduate. This time we had informed and mailed invitations to friends and family for this grand achievement, and Big Mama proudly told everybody she had told back when I initially got my

Baylor rejection letter, five years earlier!

Let me tell you how great of an achievement my Baylor commencement was. I graduated 184th out of 212 in my high school class. In other words, only 28 high school seniors knew less than I did. I knew them well. I was their leader! As for my college entrance exam scores, I had an ACT test score of 10 out of 36, and an SAT test score of 700 out of 1200. I could not see before why Baylor University did not want me in the freshman class, but I do now. As a matter of fact, my poor class rank and extremely low college admission test scores would have blocked my admission to most colleges and universities throughout the country.

Based on my 184 out of 212 high school standing, my 10 ACT score and my 700 SAT score, a group of smart people looked at a piece of paper and made an important decision about me. They decided I was not college material. They didn't get to see my face - I looked great. They didn't get to hear my voice - I sounded pretty good. They didn't get to know me, and I was pretty cool, even back then. Instead, they judged me on one piece of paper, the transcript.

In life, sometimes we look better on paper and sometimes we look worse on paper, than we really are. Although I am referring specifically to a high school transcript, *paper* represents us throughout our entire lives. Your *paper* might be your high school or college transcript, your resumé or vitae, or your introduction or cover letter for a job or a position. It might even be an electronic record or an online application. Whatever your *paper* might be, the reality is that your introduction is seldom in person. We are initially some form of *paper*. And if all goes well, if we look good on *paper*, we have the opportunity to make that next connection.

I contend that *paper* cannot reveal the nature of our hearts. *Paper* cannot fully convey our zeal or drive. *Paper* cannot relate or characterize who we truly are. If we plan to advance to the next level, we cannot afford to reduce our beliefs about ourselves to what's on our *paper*. We must elevate our beliefs about ourselves to what is in our hearts. I'm absolutely convinced that if you want something badly enough, you may have to overcome what's on, or not on the *paper*. Often times we must work harder than our *paper*, and look inside ourselves to find the drive that will help us achieve our goals and continue to our next, progressive step - or leap!

I must admit that my *paper* portrayed a pretty dismal picture. My high school grades indicated I was only interested in getting by. They showed a lack of effort, determination, and attention to detail and drive – in school subjects.

Had the admissions officers been able to see into my heart, they would have seen a heart that wanted a chance to prove it could achieve academic success. They would have seen the heart of a young man who studied his football playbook hours upon end until he knew his assignments very well.

My heart was full of passion and commitment in high school, but because my passion and commitment were misplaced, school work did, in fact, bore me. Had someone in Baylor admissions seen me personally, perhaps, they could have helped guide my efforts in a direction that was more realistic and beneficial for me. That chance, however, didn't come because the *paper* overshadowed my desire. Although the grades said I was getting by, I really was not getting by at all. I was doing just enough to pass. I came to this incredible realization during a life-changing trip.

It was the summer. I had graduated from Baylor, and my *paper*, I thought, was looking pretty good. I had earned my bachelor of business administration degree and accomplished that goal.

On top of that, I was about to take my first plane ride to the nation's capital. I thought life could not possibly get any better. I had reached a pinnacle of sorts. Wow, was I wrong! When I reached Washington, D. C. and began to behold with my own eyes the Washington Monument, the Capitol, the Lincoln Memorial, the Pentagon, the Smithsonian National Air and Space Museum and other testaments to our nation's historical accomplishments, my entire reality changed. My mind was racing so fast I could hardly keep up.

Had I seen Arlington National Cemetery and the Changing of the Guards at the Tomb of the Unknown Soldier before my first history class, how differently would I have responded to the academic classroom? Had I toured the Smithsonian National Air and Space Museum or any of the fabulous Smithsonian facilities before I had taken high school algebra or science, would I still have done so poorly in those classes, or would I have inquisitively listened and learned from the teaching and learning that was there all along in my classes?

Had I walked the halls of the Smithsonian before I was in high school science class, would the experiments I merely attempted have had more meaning? Had I been able to inhale the aroma of greatness that permeated the halls of the Pentagon or the Capitol before my first political science class, would I have been inspired to follow in the footsteps of the great statesmen and orators by grasping the lifelong skill sets of reading with understanding, writing with clarity, and speaking with purpose?

Would I still have cheated myself by merely doing what was necessary to get a passing grade, like I did in typing class by looking at the keyboard, instead of looking at the paper from which I was typing? That's how easy it is to just get by if you don't know what real learning is about. It's about the big picture, but you must do the little things first. The little things make the big difference.

Finally, I understood. What I found walking the halls and galleries of grandeur in Washington D. C., were some of the hows and whys and the meaning of learning and understanding. Education and learning just to make a "grade" was questionable. If I merged all my great teaching and learning, I would possibly have discovered success earlier in my education.

These days, my *paper* looks much different than when I applied to Baylor. Since that dismal rejection letter, I have earned my Bachelor and Master degrees from Baylor University, and my Doctorate degree from Texas A & M University.

When I include the adversities and opportunities in my life, along with my education and experiences, it expands the breadth and deepens the level of my commitment to spend not just my career, but my life helping others move to their next levels and pursue their goals.

50

7

Difference Maker

"All birds find shelter during a rain, but the eagle avoids rain by flying above the clouds. Problems are common, but attitude makes the difference."

-Unknown

51

There are certain people in our lives who can help us get to the next level. For me, Big Mama was that one special, influential person. She instilled in me the assurance of success, regardless of the conditions. Big Mama preached to us that circumstances wouldn't determine our success, we would. For example, even though Big Mama understood that systems could be unfair, she never got mad at the system, nor would she allow us.

Instead, she taught my sister and me that rather than get angry, we should *get smart*. To her, that meant that we should work *smart* then work hard. She didn't want us to just be content to work hard. Think about the type of work you are doing. Are you planning to do it for a long period of time? Are you doing a good job? Are you learning something new every day? Are you helping make a difference? Where do you go next?

Big Mama, with her third grade education, insisted that I learn how to communicate well with others. Leadership guru, John C. Maxwell said, "It's not enough just to work hard. It's not enough to do a great job. To be successful, you need to learn how to really communicate with others." Big Mama communicated and connected!

With her foresight, she knew that the only way we would have significant opportunities from which to select the best choices, would be through her prayers, her encouragement, and our education.

Big Mama was my strongest prayer warrior, but she was also my first and most gifted teacher. She was such a great teacher that she made even the menial task of grocery shopping seem fun. That's why I always loved hanging out with her. One of our Saturday jobs was going to the grocery store.

At the Piggly Wiggly, Big Mama and I shared many teachable moments. Perhaps the most memorable was in the checkout line.

Although I was only about 6 years old, I will never forget it. Big Mama and I were in the checkout line waiting directly behind another lady and her son. He was about my age. Their basket was as full as ours. We were content to stand and wait until it was our turn.

The lady and her son were almost finished when all of a sudden a pretty green and yellow John Deere toy tractor rolled across the checkout counter. The mother said, "No, I didn't get that; put that back." The little boy replied, "Mom, I want that." "No," she said, "you can't have that; put that back."

At this point, the little boy went from negotiation to temper tantrum. He started crying and screaming, "I want that! I want that!" He pitched a fit and made a scene. He just wouldn't stop.

Finally the mother said to the checker, "Go ahead and let him have it." When the little boy heard that, he dried his tears in no time, and all was happy and right with his world.

I was standing next to Big Mama watching this all unfold.

She turned to me.

"Bennie!"

"Yes ma'am, Big Mama?"

"Did you just see what that little boy did?"

"Yes ma'am, Big Mama."

With purposefulness and deliberateness, Big Mama took the strap of her purse and began to spank me – emphasizing each syllable with an accompanying swat.

"DON'T-YOU-EV-ER-DO-THAT!" Big Mama spanked me for that kid, and I didn't even know him.

I was just an innocent bystander. Incidentally, every time I go home, I still look for that kid. I need to let him know that on a Saturday morning at the Piggly Wiggly grocery store, I received a spanking for him from Big Mama!

What Big Mama taught me that day was an important life lesson. It's been said that a doctor does not have to have your condition or ailment in order to help you. Big Mama used that teachable moment to make sure I would never even consider such inappropriate behavior as the young boy in front of us displayed. Believe me, after Big Mama finished disciplining me, I was clear.

That single lesson has prevented many an ill-fated decision or action over the years. That's why my Big Mama was that one special, influential person in my life. Not only does her spirit still flourish in me, but so do her life lessons. In each of us, one or two spirits or personalities stick with us and influence us daily. You only need one person to inspire you, to encourage you to never hang your head, to exhort you to lift up your eyes and to be grateful.

These special, influential people enable us to see our purpose and what we can become. They caution us to be thankful for what we have and even for what we don't have. Everybody in your life will not be this for you or to you, but you only need one. Let's take a look at our feathered friends to emphasize this point.

Have you ever noticed or observed the habits of an eagle? The eagle is indeed a rare and special bird. As the eagle flies, it soars and rises to the highest level of flight. It does so very gracefully and naturally.

However, in order for the little eaglet to learn to fly, the process is one of trial and experience from the start. You have to understand how a young eaglet is taught to fly. The mother eagle takes her young eaglet with her on flight, then once the mother eagle reaches the appropriate height, she drops the eaglet in hopes the young newborn will begin to flap its wings while in the air.

Unfortunately, the young eaglet does not. The mother eagle then swoops down from the sky to catch her young eaglet before it hits the ground. The mother eagle repeats this process over and over - soars to the appropriate height in the skies with her young eaglet and finally drops her again hoping the eaglet will begin to flap its wings and soar like the eagle it was born to be.

The mother eagle has to swoop down again just before her eaglet hits the ground to save it from harm. The process is repeated, until finally the eaglet, after being dropped from the sky by its mother, begins to flap its wings for the first time. The young eaglet quickly realizes it can *fly like an eagle*! The young eaglet can soar.

The amazing lesson learned from analyzing how young eagles are taught to fly is that they always possessed everything they needed to fly. They had it within them all along, but they would not have used their wings to fly if their mother had not taken them to the highest heights and dropped them. This forced them to utilize the pressure of the wind in their face, to flap those God-given *tools* called wings to make their life journey self-sufficient and fulfilling as an eagle. Hence, the only birds that soar with eagles are other eagles.

Do you want to associate with other people who carry themselves personally and professionally as an eagle? Make a list of the people in your life who are *eagles* in your mind. What is it they have that attracts you to them? Are you associated with them? What would you need to do differently to be associated with *eagles* in your life?

Just like the newborn eaglet, flying was within him at birth. I would suggest and submit to you that the tools for you to be an *eagle* are within you too! Just as the eaglet needed that one special person, mama eagle, to help him reach the goal of flying, each of us need a "Big Mama" to nudge or even push us to our next level.

BENNIE LAMBERT, Ph. D.

8

Attitude Matters

"Ability is what you're capable of doing.
Motivation determines what you do.
Attitude determines how well you do it."

-Lou Holtz

Because you never get a second chance to make a first impression, your attitude and behavior count! Let me illustrate. Some friends of mine in a major city had a son whose eligibility to play high school basketball was in question. Their son, Raul, was an outstanding athlete who had started on the varsity team for three years. Due to an ambiguous rule by the high school state governing board, Raul was told he would not be eligible to play basketball his senior year.

Needless to say, Raul, his parents, teammates, the fans, and especially the coach, were not happy about this news. Raul could have chosen to give up, accept the ruling by the board and spend his senior year as a spectator. Instead, Raul kept a positive attitude and decided to appeal the board's decision.

First he appealed in writing. The board responded, requesting he appeal in person at a hearing in the state capital. The appeal was held in a large room with a long table from which the 10 board members presided. When Raul, his parents, and his coach arrived, they learned that another athlete was there appealing the same ruling. Both boys were from the same area of the state. Both were rising seniors, and both were bilingual. Unfortunately, this is where the similarities ended.

The other student was dressed in baggy jeans, an oversized t-shirt and a cap that was cocked to one side. Although this student had attended school in the United States for many years and spoke English, he chose to speak his native language when answering the board members' questions.

At times he would switch back and forth, using both languages incorrectly. The board had to use a translator to communicate the student's responses. The student sat slouched in his chair, often shrugged when the board asked a question, and overall, had what appeared to be an *I could not care less attitude*. However, I assume he did care because he was there, after all, appealing the decision.

My friend's son, Raul, was dressed in a suit and tie, and had a fresh haircut. He sat up straight, looked the board members in the eye when he spoke, and answered their questions with "yes sir" and "yes ma'am." Additionally, he had prepared a folder for each board member with copies of his report cards, results from the mandated state tests, school attendance records, and letters from his teachers attesting to his good character. Although English was his second language, he spoke in English and translated for his parents who were not as fluent in English.

Two young men: same situation, same background with different attitudes and with markedly different outcomes. One was granted permission to play basketball his senior year; one was denied. Incidentally, Raul is still playing basketball, now on the college level. It appears that this young man's positive and respectful attitude toward the board influenced the members and their decision to allow him to play varsity ball his senior year.

Attitude and behavior don't just count, they predict.

Consider the words of *Charles Swindoll:*

ATTITUDE

The longer I live, the more I realize the impact of attitude on life. Attitude to me is more important than the past, than what other people think or say or do. It is more important than appearance, giftedness or skill. Attitude will make or break a company, a church, a home, a relationship. The remarkable thing is we have a choice every day regarding the attitude we will embrace that day. We cannot change our past; we cannot change the fact that people will act in a certain way. We cannot change the inevitable. The only thing we can control is our attitudes. I'm convinced that life is 10% of what happens to us and 90% how we react to it. And so it is with you; you are in charge of your ATTITUDE.

Did you get the connection? It is not your status or station in life that determines your destiny; it is your attitude. Attitude is non-discriminating. That's why on a daily basis, I tell myself, "It's a great day!" Even if it's raining outside, it is a great day!

You get to choose your attitude every day. By keeping our attitude and self-talk positive, we can gain proper perspectives and outcomes regardless of the circumstances.

Even the word *ATTITUDE*, when analyzed mathematically, reveals its importance. Someone devised the simple test below to illustrate this point. By assigning each letter of the alphabet to a corresponding number (i.e. A = 1, B = 2, C = 3, etc.), you will discover that the word *ATTITUDE* mathematically adds up to 100.

<u>A</u> = 1, <u>T</u> = 20, <u>T</u> = 20, <u>I</u> = 9, <u>T</u> = 20, <u>U</u> = 21, <u>D</u> = 4, <u>E</u> =5 = **100**

I don't think it is coincidental that the word *ATTITUDE* equals 100. Those who display good attitudes typically move ahead of the pack 100 percent of the time because attitude manifests what is on the inside through behaviors on the outside. People have overcome seemingly insurmountable odds by choosing to have positive attitudes.

Albert Einstein, famous mathematician and physicist, had a learning disability and did not speak until he was 3 years old. He found math and writing difficult at school but went on to become one of the best known scientists of all time.

Franklin Delano Roosevelt, the 32nd President of the United States, contracted polio in 1921, which left him paralyzed from the waist down. Refusing to accept his paralysis, he tried different therapies and methods, attempting to regain the ability to walk, and he mastered walking short distances using iron braces and a cane. He later established a foundation to help others with polio and directed the March of Dimes, which eventually funded an effective polio vaccine.

And then, there was Big Mama. She had only a third grade education but volumes of knowledge called common sense. She managed to make sure I had all the essentials of a quality life without revealing to anyone how poor financially our family really was. Big Mama had a super positive attitude!

When we were sick or under the weather, Big Mama used her wisdom and knowledge of food and homemade medicines to heal us. When we needed appropriate clothing for school, she bought the material and made our clothes. No one even knew our clothes were handmade by Big Mama because they were so cool!

When it came to providing good, healthy food for us, Big Mama purchased basic ingredients and grew the rest of our food so we ate as well as anyone. When it came to having more than just a solid roof over our heads, Big Mama made our house a comfortable home. She always had plenty of food and a welcoming spirit, and our house was not just home for our family, but for anyone who visited. What a difference attitude can make.

As I mentioned, I rarely missed school. This was definitely because of Big Mama and her belief that learning was extremely important. However, when I would bring my report card home from school to be signed, the categories that mattered most to my family were not the grades in each subject area, but my marks in the Attendance, Attitude, and Behavior categories.

I did not know that my family was functionally illiterate until I was about to graduate. Amazingly though, they had enough common sense to realize that the secret to reaching the next level was determined more by attitude than by education.

Guess what? That's still the secret today! If we plan to move to the next level, we must practice good attitudes and behaviors, be present physically and mentally, and be an asset to our environments. Years ago, Big Mama, my special, influential person, made sure I knew this secret, and it has made all the difference in my life.

9

Moving On

"All mankind is divided into three classes: those that are immovable, those that are movable, and those that move."

-Benjamin Franklin

D o you remember your first day in high school? You've moved to the next level, but it's new and unfamiliar because . . . you are a freshman. As you look around at the upperclassmen, they seem to know what they are doing, and they do it with ease. You, however, along with the other freshmen, stumble and fumble about like the inexperienced high school student that you are. You find yourself lost, unsure, making mistakes, and at times, totally clueless. How could this be? You just advanced to the next level!

It's your first day in college. You've moved to the next level, but it's new and unfamiliar because . . . you are a freshman. As you look around at the upperclassmen, they seem to know what they are doing, and they do it with ease. You, however, along with the other freshmen, stumble and fumble about like the inexperienced college student that you are. You find yourself lost, unsure, making mistakes and perhaps, totally clueless. How could this be? You just advanced to the next level!

It's your first day on the job. You've moved to the next level, but it's new and unfamiliar because . . . you're the new guy on the job. As you look around at the tenured employees, they seem to know what they are doing, and they do it with ease. You, however, stumble and fumble like the inexperienced new hire that you are. You find yourself lost, unsure, making mistakes and perhaps, totally clueless at times. How could this be? You just advanced to the next level!

Are you sensing a pattern here? You will find that life is a lot like being a freshman in high school. Whether you move from eighth grade to ninth grade, high school to college, or college to your first professional job, you will always be the new kid on the block. Moving to the next level brings with it, by necessity, unfamiliarity and a learning curve; however, just like you learned the ropes in high school by the time you were a sophomore, you will eventually learn the ropes of every new level you attain.

At any level you are prone to making mistakes because of the lack of immediate experience and knowledge in that particular environment; but over time, with the proper training and assistance, rookie mistakes become a thing of the past, and the rookie, himself, becomes a reservoir of experience and knowledge.

Knowing and expecting the newness of the freshman/rookie experience can ease the tension for you and allow you self-confidence to succeed at your new next level. The freshman/rookie experience is an important phase in growth. It's in this phase that we focus on learning, experience, and progress. While we are in the freshman/rookie phase of our lives, we should take advantage of the assistance, advice, and support of those more experienced around us. Those who have been where we are can be invaluable to our success as we strive to master our new areas, skills, and responsibilities.

I used to shy away from joining certain clubs or organizations. I didn't understand they were platforms for moving to new levels. Initially I deemed them elitist, but after understanding my need to move to the next level, I took a deeper look. What I saw were people who had chosen to associate themselves with others of similar goals and beliefs.

Members of groups typically share common ambitions for themselves, their families, and their communities. They tend to encourage each other to attain higher levels of responsibility, service, achievement, and accomplishment. I realized that the members of these organizations nurtured dreams and desires that I didn't even know existed.

I had stunted my own growth by succumbing to the *birds of a feather flock together* mentality, limiting my interaction to only those who thought, talked, and lived like I did. This existence proved ineffective when I wanted to move to the next level. I discovered that in order for me to reach a higher level, I had to align and associate myself with those who were already at higher levels than I.

I have a friend who went to the gym religiously to work out for many years. Rain or shine she was on the elliptical and did an hour of cardio daily. Not only did she feel comfortable with her workout, but she felt comfortable with her body, as well. One day a friend suggested she try weight training. Her initial response was, "No, thank you."

After a few days of urging, she reluctantly decided to give weight training a try. She found that weight training forced her to use muscles that she had not used at all on the cardio machines, and she had the soreness to prove it.

Despite the aches and pains, however, she continued with the weight training and within a few weeks saw definite improvements in the way her body looked and felt. Today she has a very balanced workout, alternating between cardio and weight training.

Hence, the one hour of cardio she did everyday was fine, but by not doing the weight training, she was limiting herself and her body. So many times in life, we limit ourselves because of experiences and activities that we are not even aware of. We often go through life with blinders on, oblivious to the great things that are happening in the same room with us.

I found my experiences in broadening my associations to be much like my friend's exercise experience. Although I encountered, and continue to do so with each new association, the freshman/rookie phase like she did with her sore muscles, I found the capacity for growth well worth the awkward and often uncomfortable transition period.

I encourage you to purposely move to the next level by changing your associations. I have provided a *starter* list of ways that you can begin to change your associations.

Volunteer: Through volunteering, you can bring your natural gifts and talents to the table - or you can bring yourself, along with a positive attitude, and learn how to do something new that will help others and add to your own skill set and life.

Participate in civic, social, and other faith-based organizations: Attend events, read local newspapers, websites, magazines, and publications to discover which scheduled events and attractions spur your interest, desire, and passion. Follow up with the contact person for the location, time, and date. Ask if any additional help is needed to support the event.

Enroll in classes at a local community college: Community colleges are the least expensive, highest quality, personal development venue for higher education and training beyond high school. More than 60% of all people enrolled in colleges and universities in America today are in community colleges. Even those who have already earned a degree take classes at community colleges to pursue new interests and learn new skills.

Advance your education and learning: We live in the greatest country in the world, the United States of America. The access to training and higher education is accessible and available for almost everyone who desires to learn more and do more. I wholeheartedly believe that college is NOT for everybody, but EDUCATION is; therefore, do not limit yourself. Explore your options! The options are endless. Do your homework!

Really get to know people outside your neighborhood: We are all initially creatures of habit. You have to purposely break habits. It is not uncommon for people who travel to foreign countries for the first time to look for a familiar place to eat. For example, an American who vacations in London might eat his first meal at a familiar restaurant like McDonald's. You should purposely break the habit. Take the first step. Go where the people of that community go. Engage the locals!

Read, Read, Read: The keys to taking it to the next level are simple: keep growing, learn new things outside of your comfort zone, move, travel, explore and read, read, read.

10

The Formula: L = T x R x PE

"The most important single ingredient in the formula of success is knowing how to get along with people."

-Theodore Roosevelt

There are three components that really help when moving to the next level. They are, *time on task*, *resources*, and *positive experiences*. All of these things have to be ignited, in some form or fashion, so that better things can happen. Some of us spend too much time with our gearshift stuck in park. When this happens, we start to really regress, and regression, unless you're using it in a statistics problem, is not a good thing.

I believe the following formula is the key to moving to the next level: **L = T x R x PE.**

Learning = Time on Task x Resources x Positive Experiences.

I am convinced, I don't care what one's background is – if you have enough time on task, enough resources and enough positive experiences, you can achieve it – whatever *it* is.

For example, look at the Williams sisters, Serena and Venus. Their reputation on the world tennis circuit precedes them. The question is: were these two sisters coincidentally born with the God-given talent to win almost 30 grand slams in their short lives? Or, did they become the tennis cover girls because their father handed them tennis racquets in infancy and provided them with time on task, resources, and positive feedback for them to become the stars they became?

Reportedly one of their father's favored training techniques involved putting the girls against a wall then blasting hundreds of tennis balls at them, rapid fire, to teach them to *defend* themselves with their racquets. The girls were provided with the resources, the time, and eventually the positive experiences which equated to not merely learning, but ultimately to winning titles and medals and becoming very successful at their skill.

There are countless professional athletes, musicians, actors, etc. who utilized time on task, and were provided with the significant and appropriate resources at a very young age. In these situations, for the vast majority, success is inevitable.

For those of us who were not fortunate enough to have these resources available, or in some cases, forced upon us, we have to make a conscious effort to use our imagination, energy, and resourcefulness to learn how to successfully compete with what we have.

Let me illustrate this point. A young lady desired to be an elementary teacher. She earned her teaching certificate and landed her first teaching job. In college, she graduated at the top of her class and had enjoyed a very successful student-teaching experience.

Like most first year teachers, she was not fully prepared because college cannot provide and prepare for every scenario that will happen during that first year of teaching. She did not have effective classroom management. She had difficulty organizing the students and their lessons. Parents complained about her to the administration, and she was discouraged to the point of giving up. Eventually, a veteran co-worker stepped in and *coached* the "rookie" teacher on how to better manage and organize her lessons and students. She invited the first year teacher to observe her classes and watch her teach.

She recommended practical in-services for her to attend and practical books for her to read and apply. With all of these resources, her teaching improved, as did her confidence, and she started experiencing the successes and rewards of teaching.

$L = T x R x PE$ not only applies to reading, science, and math, but to the majority of the challenges a person wants to overcome.

By the way, during my time at Baylor, the crowning moment came shortly after graduation. I received a phone call from the President of Baylor University, Dr. Herbert Reynolds and Dean Thomas. Yes, the same Dean Thomas who sent me that rejection letter in the spring of my senior year of high school that read:

> "*Dear Bennie Lambert, You have honored Baylor by applying for admission, and we sincerely appreciate your interest.*
>
> *However, due to low test scores and poor class rank, we are unable to admit you to Baylor University.*"

He and the President wanted me to work for Baylor University. Ironically, the same place that told me, "No" to my application for admission, offered me my first professional job opportunity.

Through time on task, resources, and positive experiences, I acquired the qualities that Baylor University desired. My first professional job, when I graduated from college, was working for the President of the university that initially told me, "NO" - Baylor University.

I think an important point of my story is that there will always be people who will say, "No, you can't do this," or "No, you can't be that." If you believe them, then they are absolutely correct. However, your mind has the ability to put its imagination in action, and that action has the potential to allow you to prepare a work plan with the possibility for you to accomplish anything you set your mind to. All it takes is time on task, resources, and positive experiences. When you apply these elements consistently, you will be able to pursue your passions!

Based on this formula, the Williams sisters and the rookie teacher, overcame adversity and experienced positive growth.

On the contrary, about a year ago, during a casual conversation, one of my best friends shared a true story with me. The story she shared actually happened 30 some years ago, but impacted me deeply. Her simple story is the epitome of someone, who through no fault of her own, didn't *grow from no*. Her story reinforced for me that my message is vital to helping people.

My friend's name is Angela and she is a high school English teacher. One day while teaching, the choir director stopped in her room and they proceeded to share small talk. When the conversation turned to choir tryouts, Angela told the choir teacher that as a child out of her close-knit class of 30-some sixth grade students, she was the only one who didn't make the junior high choir. Instead, she had to take a music theory class and read about music from a book.

Naturally at the tender age of 12, Angela was disappointed that she did not make the choir; but more than that she was embarrassed and even humiliated. She loved singing and was told she didn't sing well enough to make the junior high choir - not even the second string. After that, Angela stopped singing. She loved the hymns at church, but she no longer sang during mass. She loved the country songs on the radio, but she only listened - never sang along. At birthday parties she did not join in when everyone sang *Happy Birthday* and at sporting events, though deeply patriotic, she remained silent during the *National Anthem.*

Her co-worker, moved by her story, responded that she

could have learned to sing. "How?" asked Angela. He told her that as a choir director he teaches students how to sing every day. "Just like students come to you who don't know how to write, I get students who don't know how to sing. Your job is to work with them and teach them how to write; my job is to work with them and teach them how to sing."

Angela was stunned. "You mean I could have learned to sing? I could have been in the choir? I could have been singing along all these years?" The choir director affirmed her questions.

As Angela told me this story, she became emotional. She explained the unnecessary hurt she went through way back when, and more importantly how she was still, as an adult, self conscious of singing in public.

Like I said, this story hit home with me. A simple story, yet I know similar scenarios have happened to *all* of us. The lesson is, not to accept *no* for an answer but instead *break through* the adversity until we get what we want and reach our goals.

BENNIE LAMBERT, Ph. D.

11

From "Abe" to ABC

"I have learned that success is to be measured not so much by the position that one has reached in life as by the obstacles which one has overcome while trying to succeed."

-Booker T. Washington

O ne of my favorite people is a man who failed in business. He was defeated for state legislature. He tried another business a few short years later. It failed again. He ran for Congress. He was defeated. His fiancé died. He had a nervous breakdown. He ran for Congress again, and was defeated. He tried running for the Senate. He lost. The next year he ran for Vice President and lost. He ran for Senate again, and was defeated.

However in 1860, the man who signed his name "A. Lincoln" was elected the 16th President of the United States.

People often ask, "Bennie, who is your role model?" My first response is Big Mama then Abe Lincoln. Then they say, "I know why you like Abraham Lincoln, because of the *Emancipation Proclamation.*" Of course, I'm glad he did that. I'm very glad that came about.

The true reason I admire Abraham Lincoln is because he was told publicly over and over again, not just in front of family and friends, but in front of the world, that he could not do what he wanted to do. Everyone knew on *paper* that he was a failure. However, in reality he was a person who never quit.

Lincoln was told by people repeatedly, "No you can't do this; No you can't do that," and he ended up holding the highest office in the land. Lincoln is widely acknowledged as one of the greatest Presidents of this country. Very few people know what he had to go through to get there. I think it is important to know every great leader and every great person overcame some great level of adversity to achieve their goals.

Make the tough choices - Never quit! That's how you get to the next level. That's *How to Grow from No.*

It is okay to fail as long as you keep trying and learn from your mistakes. Learning is education.

Education is not a cup that runs over rather it is a cup that never fills. By the time you learn what you think you need to know, some of it will already be obsolete. Zig Ziglar said, "You have an excuse to not have a degree, but you don't have an excuse not to have an education." We should never stop learning. Education is a lot like the commercials.

- Education is like the airlines: It's ready when you are and even when you're not.

- Education is like American Express: Don't leave home without it.

- Education is like Coke-a-Cola: It's the real thing.

- Education is like Pepsi: It's the right one baby, uh-huh.

- Education is like Snickers: It Satisfies.

- Education is like Folgers: It's good to the last drop!

Education is for everyone!

We have all been exposed to education for a long, long time. People ask me, how long have you been in education? I always say since I was 6 years old - the first grade. That's how long I've been in education and for the most part, we've all been in education a lifetime. My first taste of education started with the first thing I learned - the *ABCs*. I still carry them with me today, and I still like to share them:

The ABCs for Life

A – Is for **Attitude** which determines your altitude and how high you will fly in life.

B – Is for **Brains!** You have them – use them!

C – Is for **Change**. Change your dialogue, change your environment and change your outlook!

D – Is for **Decide.** Decide you want to go to the next level.

E – Is for **Energy!** Without it nothing matters; you're just going through the motions.

F – Is for **Faith, Family, and Friends.** No one gets where they are in life by themselves.

G – Is for the **Gifts** that you have and will share with others.

H – Is for **Help.** Help someone who doesn't have what you have.

I – Is for **Improve.** Improve yourself in every aspect, every day.

J – Is for **Jackpot.** You're in America; you've hit the jackpot.

K – Is for **Knowledge** to design and follow your plan.

L – Is for **Laugh!** Laughter is great medicine. Don't be afraid to laugh – especially at yourself!

M – Is for **Miracles** – do you believe?

N – Is for **Never** quit learning.

O – Is for **Octane** to fuel your high energy.

P – Is for **Praise.** Start giving it!

Q – Is for the **Questions** you must always be willing to ask.

R – Is for **Roots.** Remember your roots determine your routes.

S – Is for **Success** - the only place the word success comes before the word work is in the dictionary.

T – Is for **Treat** others the way you'd like to be treated.

U – Is for the **University** of Life – we're all learning together.

V – Is for **Visualize** your plan.

W – Is for **Wisdom** is all around you – take advantage of it.

X – Is for **X-ray.** X-ray people, places, and things.

Y – Is for **Yes** – yes you can! Sí se puede!

Z – Is for **Zealously** strive to reach your Zodiac peak!

There is no end to what you can do or become if you keep educating yourself. While there is time, make it your aim to reach the highest goal possible. In order to keep growing, you must keep learning. Your mind, body, and spirit continue to grow as you continue to learn. Age is just a number. Learning is a lifetime experience. Never stop educating yourself. Go to your dreams; go to your next level.

Regardless of your adversities, hurdles, or roadblocks in life, you can *Grow from No*.

BENNIE LAMBERT, Ph. D.

About the Author

D r. Bennie Lambert is an engaging motivational speaker who has spent the last several years traveling the country promoting higher education and helping others reach their potential and their dreams. Through his humorous tales of personal experiences, he motivates and inspires his audiences while delivering a powerful lesson. Dr. Lambert is a maverick in the higher education arena and has a sincere desire to help people of all ages and from all walks of life. Additionally, he has helped countless companies and institutions improve productivity and morale in the workplace. If you or your organization would like to hear more from or learn more about Dr. Bennie Lambert, please visit his website at **www.bennielambert.com**

Notes:

Notes:

Notes:

Notes: